# Climbing
# Everest

## By Susan McCloskey

Series Literacy Consultant
**Dr Ros Fisher**

Pearson Education Limited
Edinburgh Gate
Harlow
Essex CM20 2JE
England

www.longman.co.uk

ISBN 0 582 84149 6

Colour reproduction by Colourscan, Singapore
Printed and bound in China by Leo Paper Products Ltd.

The Publisher's policy is to use paper manufactured from sustainable forests.

The following people from **DK** have
contributed to the development of this product:

**Art Director** Rachael Foster

Martin Wilson **Managing Art Editor** | **Managing Editor** Marie Greenwood
Clair Watson **Design** | **Editorial** Julie Ferris
Marie Ortu **Picture Research** | **Production** Gordana Simakovic
Richard Czapnik, Andy Smith **Cover Design** | **DTP** David McDonald

**Consultant** Simon Adams

**Dorling Kindersley would like to thank:** Peter Bull for original artwork. Lucy Heaver for editorial assistance. Ed Merritt for cartography.
Rose Horridge, Gemma Woodward and Hayley Smith in the DK Picture Library. Johnny Pau for additional cover design work.

**Picture Credits:** Alamy Images: Jon Bower 14b; Alpine Club Library: G.I. Finch 9tr, Geoffrey Winthrop Young 7t, Somervell 10tl; Corbis:
Bettmann 24bc, 27r, Jose Fuste Raga 25b, Robert Holmes 19, WildCountry 15t, Wolfgang Kaehler 16b; Mary Evans Picture Library: 6tr, 24cl;
John Frost Historical Newspapers: 24cla; Hedgehog House, New Zealand: 5t; Hulton Archive/Getty Images: 3bc, 14t, 15b, 24bl;
Military Picture Library: 7b; Mountain Camera / John Cleare: 1, 3br, 5br, 6b, 16t, 28b, 28t, 30t; National Geographic Image Collection: 9tl;
S. Noel: 10tr, 11, 12t; Pa Photos: DPA 13t; EPA 3bl; Royal Geographical Society: 8t, 12l, 17, 18t, 20b, 21l, 22, 23; Steve Razzetti 26b;
Salkeld Collection: 8b; Swiss Foundation for Alpine Research: 18b; Junko Tabei: 25t, 26t, 27bl, 29b; Vin Mag Archive: 24t.
Jacket: Corbis/Galen Rowell (front t); S. Noel (back); Junko Tabei (front bl).

All other images: DK Dorling Kindersley © 2004. For further information see www.dkimages.com
Dorling Kindersley Ltd., 80 Strand, London WC2R ORL

# Contents

George Mallory        Edmund Hillary and Tenzing Norgay        Junko Tabei

# The Ultimate Challenge

Imagine climbing Mount Everest, the highest mountain in the world at 8,850 metres. Numbing cold, steep icy peaks and harsh weather make Everest one of the most dangerous mountains for climbers. Raging storms can move in on howling winds with no warning, dumping 3 metres of snow on the ground. The air is so thin high on the mountain that many climbers suffer from altitude sickness, a lack of oxygen that robs the brain of its ability to think and makes even the strongest person feel weak and sick. Climbers on Everest injure themselves in falls, lose fingers and toes to frostbite, and are buried in avalanches. More than 170 people are known to have died on the mountain. Still, people continue to attempt the climb.

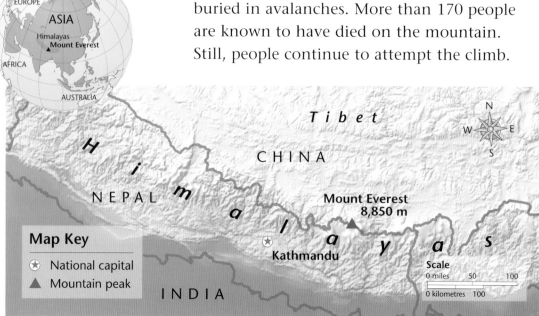

Mount Everest is in the Himalayan Mountains, on the border of Tibet, which is part of China, and Nepal.

Mount Everest is nearly 9 kilometres high.

Why would anyone risk such dangers to climb Everest? George Mallory was a famous British mountaineer who made several attempts to climb Everest during the 1920s. For him, Everest was the ultimate test of his endurance.

This book is about four people who dared to challenge Everest. They tested their strength to the limit. They all faced terrible hardships and setbacks. Yet they were all determined to stand on the summit of Everest. All but one of them made it there and back alive.

## Sir George Everest

In 1849, a crew of British surveyors mapped and measured Mount Everest and later declared it to be the highest peak in the world. In 1856, the mountain, called Chomolungma by the people of Tibet, was renamed after Sir George Everest, who spent twenty years of his life leading the effort to map India.

# George Mallory
## A Passion for Climbing

George Mallory was born in England in 1886. He had a brother and two sisters. As children, they spent a lot of time outdoors.

Young Mallory loved adventure. When he was eight or nine years old, he wanted to find out what it felt like to be on an island. So he climbed up on a big rock in the sea during low tide. When the tide came in, he was stranded and had to be rescued. His family was upset, but Mallory thought it was a great adventure.

Mallory was daring and adventurous even as a child.

When Mallory was fourteen, he joined a school mountain-climbing club. He really enjoyed climbing and went to the club regularly. When Mallory was eighteen, he climbed the Alps with the club.

Mallory climbed the Dents du Midi mountain group in the Alps.

On that trip Mallory developed altitude sickness, but it didn't stop him. He had discovered a passion for climbing. That next summer he returned to climb the Alps.

After leaving university in 1910 Mallory became a teacher. Then in 1914 Mallory married Ruth Turner, and they had two daughters and a son. In 1916, during World War I, Mallory joined the army. He worked as an officer in an artillery unit – a group that uses heavy guns to bombard the enemy.

Mallory discovered a passion for climbing on his trips to the Alps.

Mallory's artillery unit fought in France for most of World War I.

## Climbing Equipment

Early climbing equipment was very basic. They didn't have the lightweight materials that we take for granted. This made the achievements of early climbers even more impressive.

After Mallory left the army, he continued to mountain climb in his spare time. In 1921 Mallory received an extraordinary offer. A British group was planning to explore Mount Everest and climb to the top. No one had ever reached the summit successfully before. Mallory was asked to join the expedition, and, of course, he accepted.

George Mallory and his wife, Ruth

# The First Two Expeditions

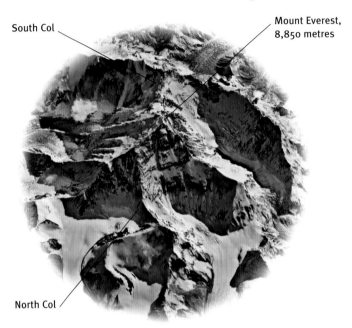

South Col

Mount Everest, 8,850 metres

North Col

Everest's north-east side includes perilous ridges.

## Base Camp

Climbers ascend Mount Everest in stages, setting up a camp at each stage. The camps help them to move equipment up the mountain in short hikes and to get used to higher altitudes. Usually it takes one to two days to adapt for every 610 metres of elevation. Base camp is the lowest one on the mountain. Mallory's base camp (above) had a few tents for the expedition's crew and supplies.

Mount Everest's peaks are connected by snow-covered ridges or passes called cols. Mallory explored and charted a route to the summit from the north-east side of the mountain at North Col – a ridge about 7,010 metres high. However, howling winds blew deep drifts of snow across the trail, and the climbers were forced to give up.

The next year, in 1922, Mallory joined another expedition. This group climbed to 8,320 metres – the highest anyone in the world had ever been. Again, bad weather stopped them from going any further.

Mallory (left) climbing in 1922

### The All-Important Sherpas

Sherpa is the name of a group of people who live in the highlands of the eastern Himalayan Mountains. Sherpa is also the name of the language they speak. Because Sherpas live in a part of the mountains in which everything must be carried by hand, they learn at an early age to carry heavy loads with ease. They're also used to working at high altitudes. Sherpas have been climbing Everest for decades.

Mallory refused to be defeated. He wanted to make one last effort before going home. On 7th June 1922 he set off for the top with fourteen members of the Himalayan mountain people known as Sherpas. They were employed as porters to carry the expedition's supplies.

The team had climbed only a short distance when an avalanche of snow roared over them. Nine men were swept off a cliff and buried under many metres of snow. Two men were dug out, but seven died.

Mallory returned home feeling heartbroken. He started teaching again and tried to forget about Everest. For almost two years, he did just that. However, in the end, he just couldn't resist Everest's pull.

# Mallory's Last Expedition

In 1924 Mallory set out again for Mount Everest. This expedition included a new member called Andrew Irvine, a strong young climber who would be Mallory's partner on the push to the summit. Early on the morning of 8th June 1924 Mallory and Irvine started out on the last leg of the climb. They carried oxygen tanks to help them breathe. Even with extra oxygen, the smallest movements were difficult at high altitudes because the air was so thin.

That afternoon, a member of the expedition below reported seeing two dots moving along a ridge towards the summit. He was sure the dots were Mallory and Irvine. However, a cloud blocked his view. Then the weather got worse. They did not reappear, and the two men were never seen alive again.

Last seen here — Summit
Camp 6
Camp 5
Camp 4
Camp 3
Camp 2
Base camp
Camp 1

Mallory's route up the north-east side of the mountain

Andrew Irvine (far left), with George Mallory (next to him) and the 1924 expedition team

Mallory and Irvine set off for the last leg of the climb.

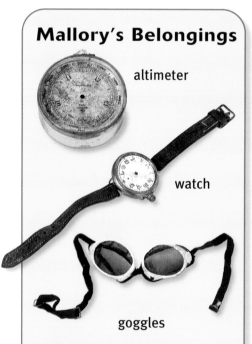

## Mallory's Belongings

altimeter

watch

goggles

These items were among those recovered from Mallory's body. Mallory's camera has never been found. Experts say that the film may still work, given the cold weather on Everest. Perhaps it holds a picture of the men on the summit.

Seventy-five years after Mallory's last climb Conrad Anker found a body on the north-east ridge of Everest. He leaned over to look at a label inside the shirt collar. It read, *G Mallory*.

Anker thinks that Mallory must have slipped and fallen off a ledge. Mallory's snow goggles were in his pocket, so the accident probably happened after dark. Mallory's rope was cut in two, perhaps by a sharp rock. His body was left on the ridge and covered with rocks. Irvine's body has never been found.

Did Mallory and Irvine ever reach the summit? Mount Everest might never reveal the answer. Still, it was an enormous achievement to climb as high as they did.

# Edmund Hillary and Tenzing Norgay
## Reaching for the Sky

Edmund Hillary was a beekeeper from New Zealand. Tenzing Norgay was a Sherpa climber from Nepal. Together, they made history.

Tenzing and Hillary

## Edmund Hillary

Edmund Hillary was like Mallory in one important way. He had always dreamed of adventure. Hillary was born in Auckland, New Zealand, in 1919. He said, "I was a restless, rather lonely child, and even in my teens I had few friends."

Hillary went to school with much older children. He was smaller than his fellow students and not very good at sports. He spent his spare time reading and imagining adventures for himself.

When he was sixteen, Hillary travelled to New Zealand's Mount Ruapehu (roo-uh-PAY-hoo). There he saw snow for the first time in his life. He skied and fell in love with the snowy mountains.

Mount Ruapehu, New Zealand

When Edmund Hillary was twenty, he went on a trip to the mountains. He heard some young men talking about climbing to the summit of Aoraki – New Zealand's highest peak. So the next day, he hired a guide and climbed his first summit. From then on, he spent his free time climbing.

At twenty-two Hillary joined the air force. He was the navigator on search-and-rescue missions in World War II. After he was badly burned in a boating accident, however, he left the airforce. He returned home and helped his father in the family beekeeping business. However, it didn't take long for him to become bored so he headed for the mountains once again.

In 1950 Hillary travelled to Europe to climb the Swiss Alps. Then he went to the Himalayas. In 1953 he joined an expedition to climb Everest. Another man in the expedition was a Sherpa from Nepal. His name was Tenzing Norgay.

Edmund Hillary served in the New Zealand Air Force during World War II.

Aoraki is also known as Mount Cook. It inspired Hillary to become a climber.

# Tenzing Norgay

Tenzing Norgay (TEN-zhing NOR-gay) was born in Tibet in 1914. He grew up in a stone house in Thamey, Nepal, only one day's walk from the base of Mount Everest. Tenzing had twelve brothers and sisters. When Tenzing was a baby, a holy man said that he was destined for great things. That's when Tenzing was given the name *Norgay*, which means "fortunate".

Tenzing grew up at the foot of the Himalayan mountains.

There was no school for Tenzing to go to. Instead he spent his childhood working as a farmer with his family. He said, "What I liked best as a boy was to go out with the yaks and wander free and alone among the mountain slopes."

**" I would sit alone and dream of far places and great journeys. "**

— *Tenzing Norgay*

Tenzing always had an adventurous spirit.

15

Mount Everest has been known by many different names throughout history.

Kathmandu, Nepal

Tenzing could see the tallest mountain in the world in the distance. Early in his life, he knew Mount Everest by the name the people in his village used: Chomolungma. His mother called it "the Mountain So High No Bird Can Fly Over It".

Tenzing was restless, just like Hillary. He said, "Always as a child, a boy, a man, I have wanted to travel, to move, to go and see, to go and find." When he was just thirteen, he travelled to see Nepal's capital city of Kathmandu – without his parents' permission. He went for six weeks. He said, "My parents were so glad to see me again that they hugged me. Then when they finished hugging me, they spanked me."

# Tenzing Norgay Earns a Reputation

In 1932, when Tenzing was eighteen, he left home with twelve other Sherpas for Darjeeling, India. This is where most expeditions to Everest began. Eventually, he became a porter for mountain climbers. He trained for his job by carrying a rucksack full of rocks up and down the hills near his home.

In 1935 Tenzing made his first trip to Mount Everest. He also joined Everest expeditions in 1936 and 1938. He became known as a dependable and hard-working porter who could carry between 27 and 40 kilograms on his back. All this time, he dreamed of climbing further and further. He said that it was "a dream, a need, a fever in the blood".

Sherpa porters carry heavy loads at high altitudes.

During World War II, the expeditions stopped. Tenzing was out of work. However, after the war, in 1952, he joined a Swiss expedition to Everest. This time, he did not go as a porter but as a climber. His wife didn't want him to go, but he could not stay away. He said, "The pull of Everest was stronger for me than any force on Earth." During this trip Tenzing and another climber came within 250 metres of the summit – the closest anyone had come yet.

Darjeeling, India, was a town where many Sherpas gathered to find work as porters.

Tenzing (right) with Raymond Lambert, a member of the 1952 expedition.

# Hillary and Tenzing Climb Together

In 1953 a British team to Mount Everest was set up which included Edmund Hillary and Tenzing Norgay. This climb was planned for the south side of the mountain. First the expedition had to hike to the base camp. This was a 320-kilometre trek from Kathmandu, Nepal. From there the team would set up camps at higher and higher altitudes. Then they would return to rest at base camp where the air was not so thin.

To establish camps higher up, the group had to climb repeatedly over the Khumbu (koom-BOO) Icefall. This was a treacherous part of the trail blocked by big chunks of ice and split by deep crevasses, or cracks. Once when Hillary was climbing the Icefall with Tenzing, he jumped over a crevasse. He fell into empty air as the snow he landed on collapsed. Tenzing was tied to Hillary, so he quickly thrust his ice axe into the snow as an anchor. As the rope pulled tight, Hillary was saved.

## What is the Khumbu Icefall?

The Icefall is part of a glacier – a gigantic, slow-moving river of ice. Its jumble of huge ice chunks is always shifting, so climbers have to adjust their routes constantly. New, deep crevasses open up unexpectedly and walls of ice often crash down. More climbers have died on the Khumbu Icefall than anywhere else on Everest.

Groups set up ropes and ladders to help them climb the Khumbu Icefall.

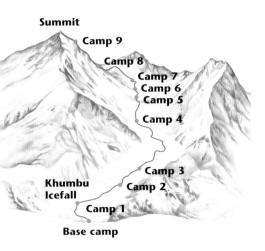

Summit

Camp 9

Camp 8

Camp 7
Camp 6
Camp 5

Camp 4

Camp 3

Khumbu
Icefall

Camp 2

Camp 1

Base camp

Hillary and Tenzing's route to the summit of Mount Everest

For the 1953 expedition the support crew laid out eight camps. Each one was higher and nearer to the summit of Mount Everest. Camp 8 was at 7,860 metres above sea level, in the area known as the Death Zone. Climbers who reach that altitude have to climb to the summit as quickly as possible, then return to a lower altitude immediately. If they don't, then they could run out of oxygen and die.

On 26th May 1953 four climbers in the expedition set out from Camp 8 towards the summit, but their oxygen ran out. They returned to Camp 8. It seemed that this camp, on the South Col, was not high enough for climbers to make it to the top and back.

Heavy equipment had to be carried from camp to camp.

So the team struggled higher and set up a new camp (Camp 9) at about 8,500 metres. Then it was Hillary and Tenzing's turn to try the climb. However, they had to wait another day because the winds were so strong.

"You don't have to be a fantastic hero to do certain things ... to compete."

*– Edmund Hillary*

Tenzing and Hillary prepare their oxygen tanks for the final ascent to the summit.

Everest summit
8,850 metres

Long-term survival impossible without bottled oxygen — 7,010 metres

Long-term living just possible — 5,330 metres

People become breathless, but adapt in two to three days — 3,050 metres

Ample oxygen

Sea level

On the night before the final ascent (28th May 1953) the temperature was –34°C with hurricane-force winds. Hillary and Tenzing tried to rest for a few hours. Tenzing said the wind sounded like "the roar of a thousand tigers". It was so cold that Hillary's boots froze. He had to use the cooking stove to thaw them out the next morning.

At 6:30 am on 29th May, Tenzing led the slow climb to the summit. Every step was an effort. Eventually all that stood between the men and the summit was a 12-metre-high rock face. Then Hillary spotted a jagged crack in the rock. He wriggled into it, and pushed himself upwards. Tenzing followed, and they kept on climbing. Finally, at 11:30 am, they reached the top.

"A few more whacks of the ice axe in the firm snow, and we stood on the top."

– Edmund Hillary, on reaching the summit of Mount Everest

Hillary and Tenzing made the final climb alone.

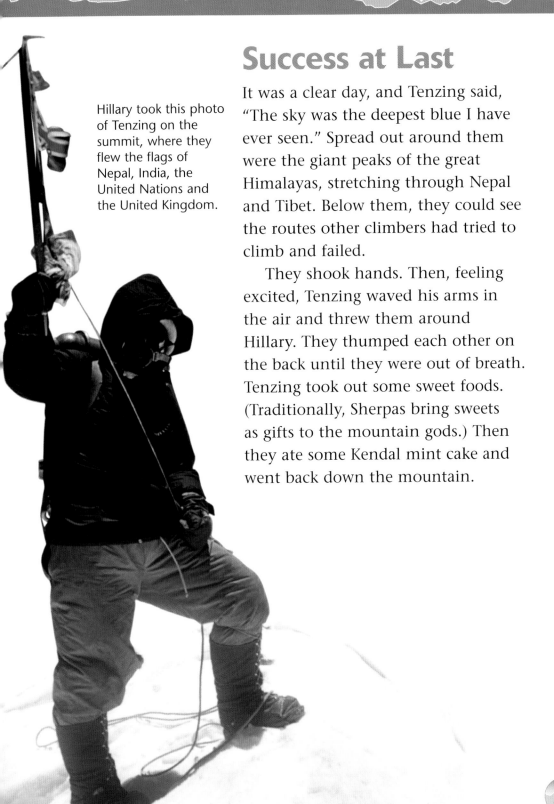

# Success at Last

It was a clear day, and Tenzing said, "The sky was the deepest blue I have ever seen." Spread out around them were the giant peaks of the great Himalayas, stretching through Nepal and Tibet. Below them, they could see the routes other climbers had tried to climb and failed.

Hillary took this photo of Tenzing on the summit, where they flew the flags of Nepal, India, the United Nations and the United Kingdom.

They shook hands. Then, feeling excited, Tenzing waved his arms in the air and threw them around Hillary. They thumped each other on the back until they were out of breath. Tenzing took out some sweet foods. (Traditionally, Sherpas bring sweets as gifts to the mountain gods.) Then they ate some Kendal mint cake and went back down the mountain.

# Tenzing and Hillary After Everest

Hillary and Tenzing became instant celebrities around the world.

The climbers were honoured with medals in Nepal and Britain.

Tenzing Norgay became a hero to the people of Nepal. After his return from the summit, he was named the first field director of a mountain-climbing school called the Himalayan Mountaineering Institute. Many Sherpas became climbing instructors through the school. Although Tenzing could not read or write, he spoke ten languages and dictated several books about his adventures. When he died in 1986, the line of people that marched behind his coffin was almost a kilometre long.

Hillary became world famous after climbing Mount Everest. However, he kept exploring. During the late 1950s he walked overland across Antarctica.

Hillary did not forget the Sherpas, whom he admired. He and his wife raised money for the Himalayan Trust, which builds schools, hospitals and clinics as well as bridges and airfields in the area. He was made an honorary citizen of Nepal during the 2003 celebration of the climb's 50th anniversary. Today, many Sherpas continue to climb the mountain, breaking records as they go. In 2002 the grandson of Tenzing Norgay made the ascent for the second time.

# Junko Tabei
## A Woman on Top of the World

Junko Tabei (JOON-koh tab-EE-ee) was born in 1939 in a small town in Japan. She was a small, delicate child who didn't like competitive sports.

When Tabei was ten, she went on a school trip to the mountains and discovered that she enjoyed climbing. She loved the beauty of the mountains, and she liked walking at her own pace. She said, "Even if you go slow, you can make it to the top."

Junko Tabei (front right) with her classmates and teacher

Mount Fuji is Japan's highest peak. It is 3,780 metres high.

Tabei spent more and more time climbing. Women weren't always easily accepted by male climbers. Sometimes men refused to climb on the same expedition with Tabei. Perhaps they felt that a woman might slow them down. So, in 1969, Tabei founded a women's climbing club. She gave piano lessons at night to earn extra money to help fund her climbing. In 1970 she made it to the top of Annapurna III. This is a difficult peak in the Himalayas.

Junko Tabei with her husband

The Annapurna range consists of six major peaks, the highest being 8,091 metres high.

# A Near Disaster

In 1975 Tabei organized an expedition to Mount Everest. It was made up entirely of Japanese women, though no woman had yet made it to Everest's summit. Early on the morning of 4th May 1975, the group was awakened by a sound like thunder. A huge wave of snow swept Tabei's tent away, with Tabei and four other women inside.

When the rumbling stopped, Tabei was in terrible pain. However, the Sherpa guides pulled her out of the snow by her ankles and saved her life. Luckily, the rest of the group survived, too.

Avalanches occur every day on Mount Everest.

Tabei led her group to the top of Mount Everest.

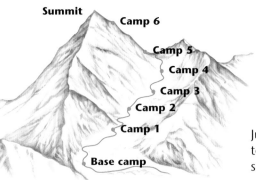

Summit
Camp 6
Camp 5
Camp 4
Camp 3
Camp 2
Camp 1
Base camp

Junko Tabei's route to the summit up the south side of Everest

Tabei on her return from the summit

Two days later Tabei could stand up again. Despite her injuries, she insisted on continuing the climb. She led her group higher and higher, sometimes walking and sometimes crawling. On 16th May 1975, twelve days after the avalanche, Tabei became the first woman to reach the top of Mount Everest.

After Tabei returned from Everest, she kept climbing. She worked for the Himalayan Adventure Trust, which works to protect the mountain environment. She has also worked to clean up rubbish left on mountains in Japan and in the Himalayas.

**"The mountain teaches me a lot of things. [It] teaches me that life should not be taken for granted."**

*– Junko Tabei*

## Mountain of Litter

As more and more people climb Mount Everest, the amount of old equipment, rubbish and unused food on the mountain increases.

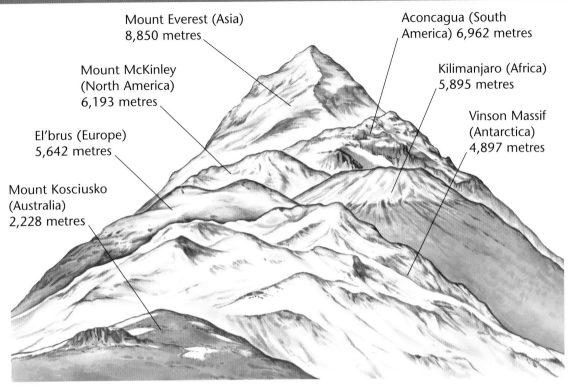

Mount Everest (Asia)
8,850 metres

Mount McKinley
(North America)
6,193 metres

El'brus (Europe)
5,642 metres

Mount Kosciusko
(Australia)
2,228 metres

Aconcagua (South
America) 6,962 metres

Kilimanjaro (Africa)
5,895 metres

Vinson Massif
(Antarctica)
4,897 metres

Tabei has climbed the highest peaks on each continent.

# Onward and Upward

Today Tabei still climbs mountains.
In 1992 she completed her goal of climbing
the highest peak on each of the seven
continents. Her next goal is to climb the
highest peak in each country in the world.

She says, "Life is not for ever. I don't
think people should leave behind a fortune,
or things. When I die, I want to look back
and know that my life was interesting.
I want to leave behind a personal history."

Tabei still enjoys
mountain climbing.

# Climbing Today

People continue to face the icy slopes of Mount Everest. Today improved equipment has made the climb more possible. Each year more than 100 climbers set out to make the ascent. New records are set only to be broken again.

Unfortunately, more climbers means more rubbish and a greater impact on the environment. Groups such as the Sagarmath Pollution Control Committee are working to teach climbers how to take better care of the mountain. With proper care, Mount Everest will continue to enchant anyone brave enough to take up the challenge.

Every year new climbers face the challenges of Mount Everest.

# Timeline

**16th May 1975**
Junko Tabei is the first woman to reach the summit.

**20th August 19**
Reinhold Messne makes the first solo ascent.

**8th June 1924**
Last sighting of George Mallory and Andrew Irvine near the summit.

**29th May 1953**
Tenzing Norgay and Edmund Hillary are the first to reach the summit.

**8th May 1978**
Reinhold Messner and Peter Habeler make the first successful ascent without oxygen bottles or tanks.

# Further Reading

*Everest*
  Rebecca Stephens (Dorling Kindersley, 2001)

*Everest – Reaching the World's Highest Peak*
  Richard Platt (Dorling Kindersley, 2000)

*Everest: The MEF 50th Anniversary Volume: 50 years
  on top of the World*
  George Band (Collins, 2003)

*Everest: The Summit of Achievement*
  Edmund Hillary (Forward), Steven Venables, Dalai Lama (Preface)
  (Bloomsbury, 2003)

*To The Top: The Story of Everest*
  Steven Venables (Walker Books, 2003)

*True Everest Adventure Stories*
  Paul Dowswell (Usborne, 2002)

**22nd May 2001**
Temba Tsheri becomes the youngest climber to reach the summit, at age 16.

**22nd May 2003**
Yuichiro Miua becomes the oldest person to reach the summit, at the age of 70 years and 222 days.

**26th May 2003**
Lhakpa Gelu Sherpa makes the fastest ascent. He reaches the summit from the base camp in 10 hours and 56 minutes.

**7th October 2000**
Davo Karnicar skis from the summit to base camp in five hours.

**15th May 2002**
Fifty-four climbers reach the summit, the highest number in one day.

# Index